KEYSTONES

Jewish SYNAGOGUE

Laurie Rosenberg

Contents

A & C BLACK • LONDON

Welcome to the synagogue!

This book is about a *synagogue* and about Judaism, the religion followed by Jewish people throughout the world. The *synagogue* is the centre of community life for Jewish people. It is a building which is used for prayer and worship, and also for education and social activities.

The children in this book wanted to find out more about Judaism. They visited a *synagogue* in Kenton, a suburb of London, together with Benjamin who is Jewish.

Benjamin met them wearing a hat called a *kippah*. He explained that boys, men and married women always make sure that their heads are covered in the *synagogue*.

Some Jewish men wear a *kippah* all the time. *Kippot* vary in shape and colour; they may be plain or decorated. Benjamin gave each of the boys a *kippah* to wear during their visit to the *synagogue*.

*The children noticed the candlestick-like sculpture on the outside of the **synagogue** building. They found out that it is a **menorah** (you can find out more about it on page 9).*

Jewish people call the *synagogue* a *shul*. This is a *Yiddish* word meaning 'school'. *Yiddish* is the language that used to be spoken by Jews in Europe. Jews used *Yiddish* so that they could speak to other Jews from many different countries. Benjamin told the children that his grandfather used to speak *Yiddish* because his parents were from Russia and Poland.

*The **synagogue** is made up of several rooms, but the most important for worship is the hall where the service takes place. The children thought that the wall of stained glass windows was very striking.*

Benjamin knows some *Yiddish* words, but this is not the language Jews use in *shul*. Like many other Jewish children, Benjamin has learned how to read and write in Hebrew. For over 3000 years, Hebrew has been the language of prayer for Jews. It is the language spoken today in Israel. As you'll see from the time-line on pages 28 and 29, Israel has had a very important part to play in Jewish history.

Being Jewish

At the *synagogue* the children met Rabbi Zneimer and Rabbi Miller who are in charge of Kenton Shul. The title *Rabbi* is only given to someone of great learning and leadership. Rabbi Zneimer told the children that, in the United Kingdom, most Jewish people live in or on the outskirts of the larger cities. Jews need to live near one another in communities which are centred around *shuls,* where they can meet and worship together.

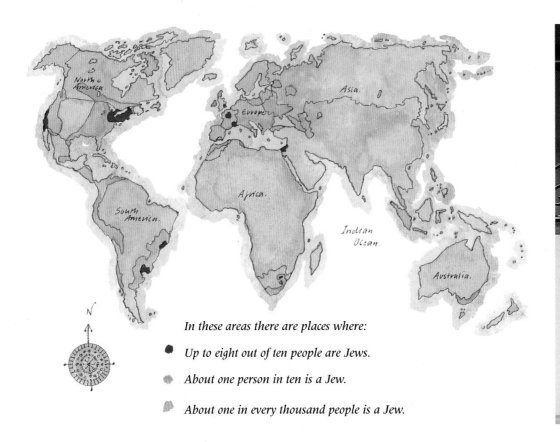

In these areas there are places where:

- *Up to eight out of ten people are Jews.*
- *About one person in ten is a Jew.*
- *About one in every thousand people is a Jew.*

This map shows where most of the Jews in the world live today. Wherever Jews live they have built **synagogues** *to help them to keep their own customs and traditions alive. However they are also proud to follow the way of life of the countries in which they have settled.*

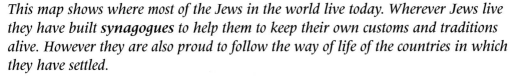

As well as *shuls*, Jewish communities are served by shops which sell special *kosher* food products. These products are made according to the laws about food which Jewish people follow. There will also be places such as nursing homes within a Jewish community where the sick and elderly are cared for.

*The children looked up their favourite foods in a **kosher** guidebook, to see whether they were suitable for Jews to eat.* ▶

*These girls explored the **synagogue** and found the ladies' gallery where the women sit during a service.*

The children in this book visited an *Orthodox shul*. Rabbi Zneimer explained that in the United Kingdom and throughout the world not all *shuls* are *Orthodox*. Some are *Progressive*.

Progressive Jews believe that the ancient laws have to be adapted to a modern lifestyle. Orthodox Jews apply the ancient laws to modern situations. For example, in an *Orthodox shul*, there are separate seating areas for men and women. *Progressive shuls* allow men and women to sit together.

How Judaism began

Judaism is a faith and way of life spanning 4000 years. The most important idea in Judaism is the belief in one God who created the world and cares for all His creation. This was first recognised by Abraham, who lived in Ur on the River Euphrates in Sumeria, in the area now known as Iraq.

Abraham believed that neither idols nor the sun (which people worshipped in those days) could have created the world. He was certain that there was an invisible and ever-present God. This idea was so odd at that time that Abraham was ridiculed and had to leave Sumeria.

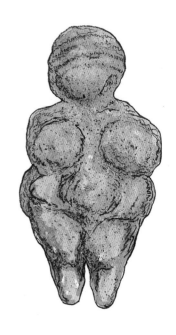

At the time of Abraham the people of Sumeria worshipped idols made of stone, clay or bronze.

This is Jericho, a city which was built in the valley of the River Jordan. It was in this area that Judaism began.

Abraham, Isaac his son, and Jacob his grandson are the three ancestors of the Jewish people today. You can read about them in the Bible. The story of Jacob's 12 children is very well known: Joseph, his favourite son, was given a coat of many colours. His other brothers were so jealous that they wanted to kill him. In the end Joseph was sold to traders who took him with them to Egypt.

Jacob became known as Israel. His children, the Children of Israel, eventually made peace with their brother Joseph, who was now famous, and joined him in Egypt. But a new Pharaoh, the ruler of Egypt, became frightened when his advisers warned him that one day he would lose his power to the Children of Israel. So he made the Jews into slaves. He even decided to have all the Jewish baby boys killed. Moses was saved by being hidden in a basket in the River Nile. It was Moses who was to lead the Jews out of Egypt to freedom.

This painting shows the Children of Israel escaping from Egypt.

The Children of Israel built the *Tabernacle* as a place of worship after their escape from Egypt. The *Tabernacle* was centred on a chest containing the *Ten Commandments*, which were handed down to Moses by God on Mount Sinai. (The Latin word for a chest is *archa*.) The chest containing the *Ten Commandments* became known as the *Ark of the Covenant*. A covenant is an agreement. Moses promised God that the Jews would keep all of the Commandments.

A link with the past

The children discovered that the design of every *shul* is based on the *Tabernacle*, which was built by the Children of Israel. Moses gave one man, Bezalel, the overall responsibility for planning and building the *Tabernacle*. It was made up of curtains and wooden pillars, and was designed to be moved from place to place. But setting up and dismantling the *Tabernacle* must have taken a long time, because it was about 50 metres long and 25 metres wide.

The building of the *Tabernacle* was the first creative act by the Jews as a community after their years of slavery. The *Torah*, the first five books of the Jewish Bible tells us that, at the time the *Tabernacle* was built, the Children of Israel numbered 600,000 people.

They were divided into different families, or tribes. These tribes were descended from Jacob's sons. The tribes camped on different sides of the *Tabernacle*. Each tribe had its own tasks and responsibilities.

At the sound of a *shofar*, or ram's horn, the leaders of each tribe would instruct their families to dismantle parts of the *Tabernacle* ready to move on.

▲ *This is an ancient drawing of the **Ark** in the **Tabernacle**.*

Looking round Kenton *Shul*, the children saw features that are a reminder of the *Tabernacle*. The *Ark* which contains the *Torah* scrolls is at the eastern end of the *shul* and is covered by a velvet curtain. The curtain is embroidered with a crown, the *Ten Commandments* and a pair of lions. The lion was the symbol of the tribe Judah, one of Jacob's sons.

*Benjamin drew aside the curtain covering the **Ark** to show the children the **Torah** scrolls.*

*The lamp above the **Ark** is called the **ner tamid**. It is a reminder of the seven-branched **menorah** that used to burn constantly in the **Tabernacle** and later in the Temple in Jerusalem.*

*The Hebrew letters above the **Ark** read "know before whom you are standing!" It is a reminder to behave properly in God's presence.*

The sacred scrolls

The instructions for building the *Tabernacle* were very precise. They are listed in the *Torah*, the first part of the *Tenakh*. The *Tenakh* is the Hebrew Bible.

The *Torah* is the collection of God's laws, commandments, rules, stories and values. It is also known as the Five Books of Moses. Jews believe that God spoke to Moses and that Moses wrote the *Torah* on a scroll which was kept in the *Tabernacle* along with the stone tablets of the *Ten Commandments*.

Rabbi Zneimer showed the children a *Sefer Torah*. The *Sefer Torah* is a scroll on which the first five books of the *Tenakh* are written. The *Torah* is very precious to Jews. Every copy is hand written on a parchment scroll using a quill pen and black ink. The scribe who writes a *Sefer Torah* copies from an exact version written in a special Hebrew script. There are no full stops or capital letters. Each *Sefer Torah* takes over a year to complete.

*The children listened to Rabbi Zneimer read from the **Sefer Torah**. They noticed that he used a pointer, made of silver. The pointer is known as a **yad**. This is a Hebrew word for hand. The Rabbi explained that he uses the pointer to make sure that he doesn't touch any of the letters. Every letter is important. If there are any mistakes or smudges, the **Sefer Torah** cannot be used.*

The children noticed that Kenton *Shul* has several *Sefer Torah* scrolls. Rabbi Zneimer explained that this is to allow the reader to read from different sections of the scroll. Each scroll is about 100 metres long. Having more than one *Sefer Torah* allows two different parts of the scroll to be found more quickly.

The scrolls are read in services in the *shul* on Mondays and Thursdays. On *Shabbat* (the Jewish Sabbath) and during festivals, the scrolls are taken out of the *Ark* to be read and carried in a procession around the *shul*. During the procession everyone stands and sings.

*These **Torah** scrolls are being carried in procession through the streets of London.*

It is a great honour to be called to read from the *Torah*. In *Progressive shuls*, both men and women can read from the *Torah*. In *Orthodox shuls* men over the age of 13 can be called upon to read from the scrolls. The first time this happens is on a boy's *Barmitzvah* (you can find out more about this ceremony on page 26).

Benjamin told the others that he will have to learn his special portion of the *Torah* to read during his *Barmitzvah*. He has to sing the words, so he is learning the age-old melody with a *Rabbi*.

*This boy is reading from the **Torah** scrolls during his **Barmitzvah**, which is taking place at the Western Wall in Jerusalem.*

What happens during a service?

Services are held every day in the *shul*. According to the *Torah*, Jews are meant to pray three times a day. The morning service is held very early, so that people can to go to work afterwards. There are also afternoon and evening services which may be held one after the other. The prayers in each of these services are the same every day. During the week a service may last for between 20 and 45 minutes. The services are longer on *Shabbat* and during festivals.

In *Progressive shuls*, the *Rabbi* usually begins and leads the service. In an *Orthodox shul*, the *Rabbi* or perhaps a member of the congregation will begin the service as soon as ten men have gathered together.

During a service, the congregation faces the *Ark*. At various times in the service, such as during certain prayers, the *Ark* is opened and the congregation stands, so that everyone is facing towards Israel. Rabbi Zneimer told the children that this helps people to concentrate on the words of the prayers.

*Rabbi Zneimer is standing on the pulpit, from where he makes speeches during a service. These speeches are mostly in English, but he will sometimes quote Hebrew passages from the prayer book, or from the **Tenakh**, the Hebrew Bible.*

The children noticed a raised platform in the middle of the *shul*. Rabbi Miller told them that this is called the *bimah*. There is a reader's desk on the *bimah* and during a service the *Torah* scrolls are read from there.

Any man can lead a service in an *Orthodox shul*. It helps if he has a nice voice, as many of the prayers are sung. There are different tunes for the prayers depending on whether they occur every day, or on *Shabbat*, or during festivals.

Shuls sometimes employ a reader with a trained singing voice, known as a *chazan* or cantor. The first ever talking film was about a *chazan*. The film was called "The Jazz Singer".

The service ends with a hymn which is sung by everyone. After the service on *Shabbat*, people meet for a drink and some cakes and biscuits. This is called a *kiddush*.

*Standing on the **bimah**, the children realised that during a service, everyone would be able to see the person reading the Torah scrolls and hear the prayers being read.*

How do Jews pray?

The Jewish book of prayers is called a *siddur*. *Siddur* is a Hebrew word meaning 'order'. The *shul* services always follow the *siddur*, so it's possible for a Jew to pray anywhere in the world and still be able to follow the service. The prayers are usually recited in Hebrew. Jewish children are taught Hebrew as soon as they are old enough to begin learning.

The most important parts of the daily services are the *Shema* and the *Amidah*. The *Shema* is the first prayer a Jewish child learns. It says: "Listen Israel. The Lord our God, the Lord is One". It is a reminder that there is only One God.

The *siddur* has all the prayers arranged in order:

1.	Daily	Morning
2.		Afternoon
3.		Evening
4.	Shabbat	Evening
5.		Morning
6.		Additional
7.		Afternoon

8. Festival services

9 Prayers for special occasions

All the prayer books follow this pattern.

*Rabbi Miller showed the children a **Chumash**. This is a book that contains the text of the **Sefer Torah**. The **Chumash** makes it easy for all the members of the congregation to follow the reading of the **Torah** scrolls. This **Chumash** is in Hebrew and English. It also contains a collection of stories and explanations to make the **Torah** easier to understand.*

◄

*This **siddur** has been written especially for children to use. Many **shuls** have a special service for children which follows the children's **siddur**. Although adults are present the children take the service themselves.*

The *Shema* prayer tells Jews to put a *mezuzah* on their doors. A *mezuzah* is a small container with the words of the *Shema* prayer written in Hebrew on parchment inside it. This reminds all Jews how important it is to pray and to teach their children about Judaism.

*This boy found a **mezuzah** on one of the door frames inside the **shul**.* ▲

The *Shema* prayer also tells all boys and men over the age of 13 to wear a *tallit*, or prayer shawl. Men wear a *tallit* in *shul*. In some *Progressive shuls* women also wear a *tallit*.

◄ *Rabbi Miller showed the children his **tallit**. This is a large wrap-around shawl, with knotted fringes on each corner. Each of the knots has a significance, relating to the number of the books in the **Torah**, days of the week and months of the year.*

Amidah is a Hebrew word meaning 'standing'. The *Amidah* prayer contains 18 blessings. It is read silently at first and then someone repeats it. This is a tradition which dates from a time when only a few people could read for themselves.

A week in the life of the shul

The *shul* is not only a place to pray in. It is also a community centre with activities for all age groups. Kenton *Shul* has classrooms and a youth club as well as a library where people come to study.

Every Sunday the *shul* runs a Sunday school, called *Cheder. Cheder* is a Yiddish word meaning 'room'. In the old days a *Rabbi* would have had a room in his house where he would teach the boys and girls. Children go to *Cheder* from the age of 4 until they are 13 years old.

*Rabbi Miller showed the children a notice board at the **shul** which gave details of activities for every age group.*

The *shul* also runs a study group for 14-18 year olds. The young people study the *Torah* and listen to guests speak on topics such as Jewish history. Sometimes they go on outings to other *shuls* and to Jewish communities in diferent parts of the country. They have even visited Israel.

Every night there are adult education classes at the *shul*. These range from *Torah* understanding groups, to *Kosher* cookery lessons.

*The children met Mrs Primhak, the **shul's** secretary. She sends out details of services, and keeps members aware of the different activities taking place at the **shul**. She also reminds families that anniversary dates of the deaths of loved ones are coming up, when prayers are said in **shul**.*

The *Rabbis* told the children that they are very keen on 'family education'. They arrange events which the entire family can take part in. Sometimes the whole congregation of the *shul* goes away to a hotel for a long weekend, usually over a *Shabbat*. These weekends give families an opportunity to learn more about being Jewish and living in a Jewish way.

There are many people without whom the *shul* would be unable to run properly. One important member of staff is a man called a *shamas*. This is a Hebrew word for servant.

The *shamas* makes sure that every visitor to the *shul* is given a seat. In an *Orthodox shul* he organises men to be called up to read from the *Sefer Torah* and puts all the books away after a service.

The *shamas* also makes sure that visitors have a home to go to on *Shabbat* – hospitality and charity towards others are very important Jewish values.

*A **shul's** most important member of staff is its **Rabbi**. Rabbi Zneimer could have had a career as a professional footballer, but chose to become a **Rabbi** instead. His diary is very full. He conducts weddings and funerals and organises education classes. Rabbi Zneimer does not lead many services, but he reads from the **Sefer Torah** on **Shabbat** and festivals.*

*The children met the members of the **shul's** Friendship Club, who gather for lunch every day, followed by an afternoon of activities.*

What happens on Shabbat?

Shabbat, or Saturday, is the most important day of the week for Jewish families. As all Jewish days start the evening before, *Shabbat* lasts from Friday dusk to Saturday nightfall. It is a day of complete rest, a reminder that God rested after creating the world, and the children of Israel rested from building the *Tabernacle*. On that day, for example, they did not make fire to melt gold.

Today, on *Shabbat*, *Orthodox* Jews similarly rest from the use of fire by not switching on any electrical appliances such as kettles, and by walking to *shul*. *Progressive* Jews take a more relaxed view of the *Shabbat* restrictions; they use electricity and may drive to *shul*.

The *shul* is very busy on *Shabbat*. The prayers are the same as on ordinary days, except that an extra *Amidah* is read.

The timetable on the next page shows what happens in an *Orthodox* Jewish home and *shul* on *Shabbat*. In the *Progressive* Jewish communities, more activities take place in *shul* than at home, but the structure of the day is the same for all Jews.

*Every **Shabbat** a different section of the **Torah** is read in order. A board in the **shul** shows the congregation which portion is to be read. In every **shul** in every country of the world the same portion is being read.*

*Whether they go to an **Orthodox** or a **Progressive schul**, most Jewish families enjoy a traditional Friday night meal together.*

HOME	SHUL

Friday morning and afternoon

Preparation: cooking, cleaning the home, setting the *Shabbat* table. Setting the time clocks so that lights will switch themselves on and off; filling the automatic urn for hot water.

Preparing the *shul*; rolling the *Sefer Torah* to the correct place; putting out prayer books. The *kiddush* is prepared for after the service on *Shabbat*.

Dusk

Candles are lit to bring light and joy into the home.

Afternoon and special evening service. The melodies of the hymns are very ancient. The *shamas* makes sure that everyone has a home to go to for the *Shabbat* meal.

Shabbat

The children are blessed. Everyone sits down at table to sing a welcoming song for *Shabbat*. Wine glasses are filled and *Kiddush* – a prayer – sung over the wine. After washing, a prayer is said over the two loaves of bread, known as *challot*. The family enjoys a traditional meal, usually of soup and roast chicken.

Sleep

After a light breakfast, the family goes to *shul*.

Home for lunch, usually with another family. *Kiddush* with wine. Wash and say prayer over *challot*. Lunch of cold meats and *cholent*, a dish of lentils, beans, onions and meat which has been cooked before *Shabbat* and kept on a slow heat in the oven.

Morning service. The weekly section from the *Torah* is read. Sometimes there is a *Barmitzvah* and a boy sings the portion. An additional service follows the *Rabbi's* speech. There is a *kiddush* with wine, cake and biscuits after the service.

The *shul* opens for afternoon activities.

Third Meal (tea, cakes, herring)

Go to *shul*.

The afternoon service includes the first part of the next *Shabbat's Torah* reading. This is followed by a learning or discussion session with the congregation and the *Rabbi*.

Havdalah

Evening and concluding service.

A candle with more than one wick is lit, to create light again. Spices are sniffed as a reminder of the sweetness of *Shabbat*. Wine is drunk and the light of the candle is extinguished in the wine to mark the end of *Shabbat*.

The Jewish year in shul and at home

The Jewish year has many festivals and special days. Most of the festivals are celebrated at home as well as in *shul*. The Jewish calendar is based on the phases of the moon. The first day of every Jewish month is the new moon. In order for the Jewish calendar to keep in step with the seasons, extra days are added from time to time according to an ancient formula. Three times in every ten years an entire month (called Adar II) is added. This is called a leap year.

THE CALENDAR	JEWISH CALENDAR	FESTIVAL	WHAT HAPPENS IN THE HOME	WHAT HAPPENS IN THE SHUL
THE HIGH HOLY DAYS:				
September/ October	1st Tishri (2 days)	**Rosh Hashanah** Jewish New Year (You can find out more about this high holy day on page 22.)	Candles are lit, wine and *challot* are eaten at a festive meal that starts with an apple being dipped in honey. In the afternoon families gather for *tashlich* by a river or the seaside, when they scatter crumbs from their pockets into the water.	The *Ark* curtain and all other covers are in white. The *shofar* is blown during the service.
September/ October	10th Tishri	**Yom Kippur:** Day of Atonement (You can find out more on page 23.)	All adults fast for 25 hours. There is a special meal at the start of the fast. Families gather together to break their fast.	The *shul* is once again all in white. The atmosphere is quite solemn and very moving.
THE PILGRIM AND HARVEST FESTIVALS				
September/ October	15 Tishri (8 days)	**Succot:** (You can find out more on page 25.) Tabernacles (9 days)	A *succah* is built and meals are eaten in it.	A large *succah* is built. Members may bring their own *etrog* and *lulav*.
	22 Tishri (9th day)	**Simchat Torah:** Rejoicing of the *Torah*.		There are special parties and singing and dancing with the *Torah* scrolls.

THE CALENDAR	JEWISH CALENDAR	FESTIVAL	WHAT HAPPENS IN THE HOME	WHAT HAPPENS IN THE SHUL
March/April	14 Nisan (8 days)	**Pesach:** Passover (You can find out more on page 24.)	The home is cleaned. Special food and utensils are used all week. The first two nights are festive *Seder* nights when people tell the story of the Children of Israel's Exodus from Egypt.	Services are held on the first and last days of *Pesach*.
May/June	6 Sivan (2 days)	**Shavuot:** Pentecost (You can find out more on page 25.)	Festive dairy meals are eaten. Cheese cake is a special favourite.	The shul is decorated with flowers and plants.

MINOR FESTIVALS

Feb/March	14 Adar/Adar II	**Purim**	Gifts are sent to friends and the needy. Street parties are sometimes held.	The story of *Purim*, in the Book of Esther is read. Fancy dress parties are held.
November/December	25 Kislev (8 days)	**Chanukah**	A happy festival, marking the time when Jews fought fiercely for the freedom to pray in the Temple. They celebrated their victory by lighting a seven-branched candlestick called a *menorah*. One day's supply of oil lasted miraculously for eight days. The *Chanukiah* is lit each day for eight days and gifts are exchanged.	The *Chanukiah* is lit each day for eight days and children's parties are held.

SAD DAYS AND FASTS

April/May	27 Nisan	**Yom Ha'Shoah:** Holocaust Remembrance day.		Services are held. Sometimes six candles are lit in memory of the six million Jews murdered by the Nazis. National events may take place.
July/August	9 Av	**Tisha B'Av:** (You can find out more on pages 28-9)	Adults fast for 25 hours	The *shul* is darkened and sad services are held.

Rosh Hashanah and Yom Kippur

Every September or October the Jews celebrate *Rosh Hashanah*, their new year. This is a very special time, when Jews think back over the past year and prepare for the next. Special prayers called *Selichot* are recited in *shul*. *Selichot* is a Hebrew word for prayers for forgiveness. The *Selichot* prayers begin the week before the Jewish New Year, in a solemn service which is held at midnight. A choir often sings during the service.

Rosh Hashanah is a very important time for the *shul*, when many more people than normal want to attend services there. At New Year everything in the *shul* is in white. The *Rabbis* wear special white robes. Even the *Ark* cover and the covers for the *Sefer Torah* scrolls are in white.

*The highlight of **Rosh Hashanah** is the blowing of the **shofar**, or ram's horn. This has been sounded by Jews for over 3,000 years. Benjamin is trying to blow the **shofar**. There is a special way to make the notes.*

*These people have gathered on a beach for **tashlich**, when they empty crumbs from their pockets into the sea as a symbol of throwing away their sins.*

Families gather together after lunch on *Rosh Hashanah* and visit a river, or walk to the beach if they live by the sea. They empty crumbs from their pockets into the water. As the crumbs float away, they remind Jews of their hope that their sins will be forgiven.

People pray hard on *Rosh Hashanah*. It is an opportunity to make new resolutions. The Jews believe that God keeps a 'Book of Life', in which good and bad deeds are written. This 'Book of Life' is opened on New Year and closed and sealed ten days later on a day known as *Yom Kippur*.

*This table has been laid for **Rosh Hashanah** with challot, wine, a bowl of apple pieces and a dish of honey.*

Yom Kippur is a very solemn day. All adults including girls over 12 and boys over 13 have to fast for 25 hours. During this time they have no food and nothing to drink, so people can only fast if they are healthy. There are services at the *shul* all day.

*This stained glass window reminds Jews that on **Yom Kippur** their good deeds will be weighed against the times when they have done wrong.*

Towards the end of *Yom Kippur* the atmosphere at the *shul* is very moving. The final service lasts for about 1½ hours. Throughout the service everyone stands and the *Ark* is kept open. At the end of *Yom Kippur* the *shofar* is sounded. Everyone is very relieved! Afterwards, families gather together to break the fast.

Pesach, Shavuot and Succot

The three festivals of *Pesach, Shavuot* and *Succot* are all mentioned in the *Torah*. They happen at different times of the year. The timings relate to the different harvests in Biblical times, when Jews flocked to the Temple at Jerusalem to celebrate the festivals.

Pesach is a spring-time festival celebrating the Children of Israel's escape from Egypt. To prepare for *Pesach* the home must be spring-cleaned. No bread products are allowed to be eaten during the festival. This reminds the Jews that when their ancestors escaped from Egypt the bread baked hard in the sun. Crackers made of flour and water called *matzot*, are eaten during *Pesach*. Special services are held in *shul* on the first two and last two days of the festival.

*Jews re-tell the **Passover** story at a special festive meal known as the **Seder** night.*

Seven weeks later the festival of *Shavuot* takes place. It commemorates the giving of the *Torah* to Moses. There is a *Torah* story that Mount Sinai was covered with flowers when Moses went up to receive the *Torah*. To remind Jews of this, the *shul* is covered in flowers and plants. In homes cheese cake and dairy meals are eaten as a reminder of how much goodness there is in the *Torah*.

*During **Succot**, some people bring an **etrog** and **lulav** to **shul**. An **etrog** is a wild citrus fruit found in Israel and Morocco. The **lulav** is made from palm branches, like those in the picture, which are bound together with willow and myrtle.*

The harvest festival of *Succot* lasts for 8 days. It reminds Jews of the time in the wilderness when their ancestors built fragile huts to shelter in.

Today, many Jewish families build a hut called a *succah*, in the garden, with a roof made of leaves and branches. Meals are eaten in the *succah*, as long as it is not too cold!

The *shul* also has a *succah*. This has to be big enough to allow all the congregation to gather inside it for a drink and something to eat after the service.

*In Israel, palm fronds like these are often used to make the roof of a **succah**.*

Family celebrations

The family is most important in Judaism. Families gather together for sad and happy times. Some of these times are part of festivals, but others relate to special times in a person's lifetime.

In Judaism girls are considered adult at 12. They are then responsible for keeping the Jewish religion. To celebrate they have a *Bat Chayil* ceremony at home or in *shul*. During the ceremony in an *Orthodox shul* the girl reads a speech based on a story from the *Torah* and receives a blessing.

*This girl is practising for a **Bat Chayil** with a **Rabbi** in a **Progressive synagogue**.*

Boys have to wait until they are 13 to be considered adult. A *Barmitzvah* marks the time when a boy is considered old enough to make up the numbers for a service. (In an *Orthodox synagogue* there must be ten men together before a full service can take place.) On the *Shabbat* nearest a boy's 13th Hebrew birthday he is called up on to the *bimah* to sing the week's portion from the *Torah*.

In *Progressive* Jewish communities both boys and girls are called up to read from the *Torah*.

In this part of the wedding ceremony, the groom is signing the marriage contract. ▼

Weddings are also held in *shul*. The *Rabbi* conducts the marriage ceremony under a canopy called a *chupah*. The *chupah* is a symbol of the home.

The couple who wish to be married stand under the *chupah*. The groom breaks a glass by stamping on it. This reminds everyone that once upon a time the Temple was destroyed. A contract is signed, then everyone has a party. The bride and groom stay for the party.

◄ *This couple are chatting to the **Rabbi** after their wedding service in a **Progressive synagogue**. They are standing beneath the **chupah**.*

When a baby is born, there are special ceremonies at home for boys and girls and naming ceremonies in *shul*.

After the death of a very close member of a family, special prayers are recited in *shul*. These prayers are called *Kaddish*. They are said at every service every day for a year after the death. They are also recited on the anniversary of the death.

*The children noticed several memorials to people while they were looking round Kenton **Shul**.*

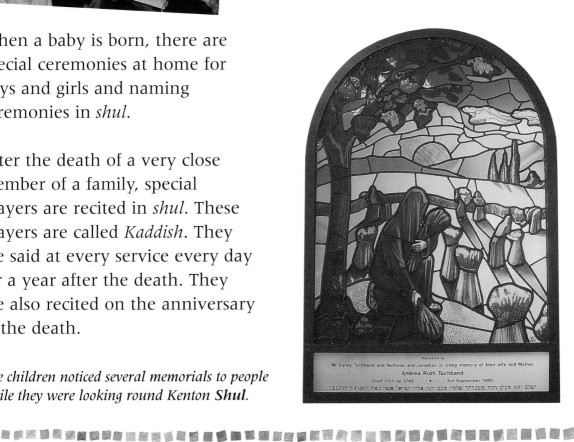

Presented by
Mr Danny Tuchband and Nicholas and Jonathan in loving memory of their wife and Mother
Andrea Ruth Tuchband
Died 30th Av 5746 - - - ◆ - - - 3rd September 1986
ישלם יהוה פעלך ותהי משכרתך שלמה מעם יהוה אלהי ישראל אשר באת לחסות תחת כנפיו

Time-line

Judaism is one of the world's oldest faiths. This time-line, which describes some of the most important periods in Jewish history, starts 2,000 years before Christianity began. These years are known as BCE (Before the Common Era). The years after this are dated CE (Common Era). This dating system is shared by members of different religions.

1000 CE
Jews settled in Europe and the Middle East.

1290 CE
Jews are expelled from England.

70CE
The second Temple was destroyed by the Romans. The Jews were dispersed throughout the world, fleeing Roman persecution.

1492 CE
The King expels Jews from Spain and Portugal

ALTNEUSCHUL, PRAGUE

1690s CE
Jews re-establish communities in England.

1880s CE
Jews establish great communities in Europe and America.

1939 – 1945
During the Second World War the Nazis murder six million Jews.

MILL STREET SYNAGOGUE, NEW YORK.
(FIRST SYNAGOGUE IN THE UNITED STATES)

2000 BCE

e time of Abraham, over
700 years ago, people
yed to the sun and used
ay idols in their homes.

The families of Jacob's
hildren settled in Egypt.

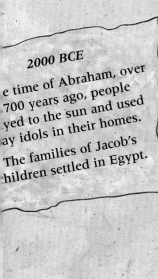

1300 BCE

The Children of Israel were enslaved by Pharaoh.
The Children of Israel escaped from Egypt into the desert.
Moses received the *Ten Commandments*.
These were originally engraved on stone tablets. They
were kept in the *Tabernacle*. The *Tabernacle* travelled with
the Jews for the 40 years they were in the desert.
Moses died and the Jews entered Israel.
Joshua became their leader.

1000 BCE

The *Tabernacle* was
set up in Jerusalem
and later a Temple
was built by King
Solomon.

168 BCE

anukah – the
dedication of
he Temple.

RAH
ESTICK

520 BCE

The second
Temple was built,
without the
*Ark of the
Covenant*.

586 BCE

The first Temple
was destroyed and
the *Ark of the
Covenant* was lost.

THE ARK

1948

fter the Second World War
ael is once again established
a homeland for all Jews, and
place where it is hoped that
ws, Muslims and Christians
ill live together peacefully.

2000

Jews have strong family values and believe
that education is very important. There are
now many Jewish schools and colleges
for children and adults, men and women
throughout the world. This is a time of
unparalleled growth in Jewish
community centres.

How to find out more

Visiting a shul

To arrange a visit to a *shul*, you should send a written request to the *Rabbi*. A list of all the *shuls* in the United Kingdom is included in the *Jewish Year Book* (published by Valentine Mitchell) which is available from your local public library.

The Board of Deputies of British Jews is the representative organisation for the entire Jewish community in the United Kingdom. Its Community Division has a section dedicated to providing authentic information on Judaism for RE teachers.

Board of Deputies of British Jews
Commonwealth House
1-19 New Oxford Street
London WC1A 1NF
Tel: 0207 543 5400
e-mail: info@bod.org.uk

As with all holy places, behaviour and dress should be respectful when visiting a *shul*. Boys should have their heads covered. You may take photographs inside a *shul*.

Things to do

You may wish to set up a Jewish corner in the classroom. You could include a *Kosher* shop (visit a Jewish shopping area to find examples of *Kosher* labels on packaging), or set a table ready for the *Shabbat* or *Seder* meals. *Challot* and *bagels* can be made out of clay and varnished. Use some fabric to make the *challah* covers which are used on *Shabbat*, together with foil candlesticks and a card *havdalah* spice box.

You could make a model of part of a *shul*, with an opening *Ark* containing miniature scrolls.

Other items in your Jewish collection could include greetings cards e.g. for a *Barmitzvah* or *Rosh Hashanah*. These are available, along with a range of other objects, by mail order from:

Religion in Evidence
Monk Road
Alfreton
Derbyshire DE55 7RL
Tel: 01773 830255

The Board of Deputies can provide guidance on the sensitive use of artefacts.

Useful words

Amidah A silent prayer recited whilst standing.

Ark The cupboard in a *shul* containing the *Sefer Torah* scrolls.

Ark of the Covenant The chest covered in gold that contained the *Sefer Torah* scrolls.

Barmitzvah The status of responsible adulthood for a Jewish boy at the age of 13, when he can be called to the *bimah* to read from the *Torah.*

Bat Chayil/Bat Mitzvah The status of responsible adulthood for a Jewish girl at the age of 12, marked by a ceremony at the *shul* or in the home.

bimah The raised platform in a *shul* from where the *Torah scrolls* are read.

Chanukah The festival during which an eight-branched *Chanukiah* is lit to recall the rededication of the Temple in Jerusalem.

Chazan A person who leads the prayers in *shul*.

Cheder The *Yiddish* word for 'room' used to describe religious education provided for Jewish children.

Chumash The *Torah* in book form.

chupah The canopy in a *shul* under which a man and woman are married.

etrog A citrus fruit which is used during *Succot*.

Kiddush In the home the *Kiddush* is a prayer recited at the start of *Shabbat* and festival meals. In the *shul*, a *kiddush* is a gathering at the end of *Shabbat* and festival services.

kippah A small covering for the head, worn by Jewish men and boys.

kosher A word describing food and other products that comply with Jewish law.

lulav Branches of myrtle and willow bound to a palm leaf, used at *Succot*.

menorah The seven-branched candelabrum used in the *Tabernacle* and Temple.

mezuzah A small box containing the *Shema* prayer, fixed to the doorposts of all the living rooms of a home and communal buildings.

ner tamid A light which is kept burning above the *Ark* in a *shul.*

Orthodox A word used to describe those Jews who apply the laws of Judaism to modern situations.

Pesach The eight-day festival commemorating the Exodus from Egypt.

Progressive A word used to describe those Jews who adapt the laws of Judaism to modern situations.

Rabbi The religious leader of a Jewish community.

Rosh Hashanah The Jewish New Year.

Seder The festive meal on the first two nights of *Pesach.*

Sefer Torah The five Books of Moses, handwritten on parchment scrolls and kept in the *shul.*

Selichot Prayers asking for forgiveness.

Shabbat The holiest day of the week.

shamas The person in a *shul* who ensures that visitors are made welcome and that the *shul* is ready for the services.

Shavuot The festival commemorating the giving of the *Ten Commandments.*

Shema The central prayer of Judaism.

shofar The ram's horn blown on *Rosh Hashanah* and at the end of *Yom Kippur.*

shul The *Yiddish* word for 'school'; a synagogue,

siddur The daily prayer book.

succah A small hut built outside a house during *Succot*, the eight-day festival held after *Yom Kippur.*

Tabernacle The portable structure built by the Children of Israel to hold the *Ten Commandments.*

tallit A prayer shawl with specially-knotted fringes at each corner.

Ten Commandments The laws engraved on stone tablets given to Moses.

Tenakh The Hebrew Bible.

Torah The core laws of Judaism, kept in the *shul* in the form of a scroll.

Yiddish The language spoken by Jews from countries in Eastern Europe.

Index

Reprinted 2002
First paperback edition 2000

First published 1998
A & C Black Publishers Ltd
37 Soho Square
London W1D 3QZ
www.acblack.com

ISBN 0-7136-5343-4

A CIP catalogue record for this book is available from the British Library

Acknowledgements

The author and publisher would like to thank Benjamin, Michael, Sarah, Sejal and Tushal and all concerned at Kenton Shul; Julie and Howard Binysh and all concerned at Bromley Shul for their generous help in the preparation of this book.

All photographs by Jak Kilby except for p6, 18b ZEFA; pp7, 8a Bridgeman Art Library; pp11a, 24, 25a,b, 26a TRIP Photo Library; p22,23a,b, Agency for Jewish Education; p27a,b Julie and Howard Binysh.

All artwork by Vanessa Card

A & C Black uses paper produced with elemental chlorine-free pulp, harvested from managed sustainable forests.

Printed in Hong Kong by Wing King Tong Ltd